BASEBALL, SNAKES, AND SUMMER SQUASH

Baseball, Snakes, and Summer Squash

Poems About Growing Up

Donald Graves

WORDSONG

WordSong
An Imprint of Highlights
815 Church Street
Honesdale, Pennsylvania 18431
Printed in the United States of America

Library of Congress Cataloging-in-Publication Data

Graves, Donald.
Baseball, snakes and summer squash: poems about growing up / by Donald Graves; drawings by Paul Birling.—lst ed.
[80]p. : ill.; cm.
Summary: The author takes an unsentimental look at his childhood in this collection of poems for young people.
ISBN 978-1-56397-530-1 (hc) • ISBN 978-1-56397-570-7 (pb)
1. Children's poetry, American. [1. American poetry.] I. Birling, Paul, ill. II. Title.
811.54—dc20 1996 AC
Library of Congress Catalog Card Number 95-60725

First edition
Book designed by Tim Gillner
The text of this book is set in Caslon 540 Roman.
The drawings are done in pencil.

10 9 8 7 6 5 4 (hc)
25 24 23 22 21 20 (pb)

To: Margaret, Sara, Joseph, Andrew,
Gregory, and Geoffrey

—DG

Contents

First Baseball Glove

"Stee-rike," George yells.
I pitch the tennis ball;
George catches.
"Baw" he says just
like he's heard
the umpires say in Yankee Stadium.

Dad comes downstairs
from our city apartment
and watches for a minute
while we throw the tennis ball.
"Come with me," he says.

"We're goin' to Sears."
He sounds excited.
He walks fast
like he's going places
and he can't wait to get there.

We go straight past toys to sports.
"Here's a catcher's mitt, George."
You're the catcher.
"Don, here's a fielder's mitt.
Try it on; see how it fits."

We race home and toss a ball
back and forth;
we yell and shout,
make the calls
with a hard baseball,
real leather mitts;
we race upstairs
to show them to Mother.

Her eyes grow dark,
she breathes deeply,
her mouth open
like she's trying to find words,
any words, and she looks
straight at Dad.

"You didn't spend
the food money, did you?"
Dad looks at the floor
like he's had a hard life.
"Time the boys had gloves."

"You boys go downstairs
while we talk," Mom says.
We play one more game
on the sidewalk,
whipping the ball,
feeling the sting
smart in the pocket.

The New Land

In fourth grade
we move from our second floor
city apartment, sidewalks,
dirt and noise,
to a house
in the country
with an apple tree,
a big yard,
and a run-down shack
we can make into a clubhouse.
Our dog, Rags,
sniffs the grass
and wags her tail.

The first morning
I look out the window
at tall fir trees
and an inlet
that reaches
in from the sea.

I set out to explore
the land, find the water;
I walk down a road,
across railroad tracks,
and up a high bank.
I follow an avenue of trees,
then poke down a path
past mosses and briars,
sweet-smelling bushes.

A puff of southwest wind
brings the sharp smell
of low tide
and through an opening
of red-leafed sumac,
I see the dark blue waters
of the inlet.

The shore is empty
except for two sandpipers
poking the beach for food.
I pick up a thin rock
and skip it
across the water.

Rags

We have a little Scotch terrier
named Rags, with hair
covering two brown eyes
that know what they want.

When we take a trip
Rags is in the car
and then in the front
seat before we
can claim our places.

She kicks her dish
against the side of the door.
We scurry like mice
to get food before
she does it again.

And when we travel to Grandmother's,
Rags stands high on the seat
as if she's driving
and makes loud sniffs
when she smells salt water
to announce we've arrived.

I read a book;
she pushes it away
as if to say,
"Let's go out."

I go into the kitchen,
quietly lift the lid
of the cookie jar
and take an oatmeal raisin cookie.
Rags barks for a piece of cookie
and the whole house
knows I've been stealing.

Rabbit

"Hey, Rabbit, come here."
I am the new kid
in the fourth grade.
My ears grow warm and large.

Sometimes I look
at them in the mirror
but not for long.
My Dad says, "Heavens,
he's got ears just like me."

In the spring, Jimmy and me
build a hut in the woods
and he says,
"Hey, Rabbit, you build
cool huts; how'd you know
how to do that?"

That night
after I brush my teeth,
I take another look
at my ears and I think
maybe they've shrunk.

THE BULLY

Bobby Nelson is the toughest kid in our class;
I am the smallest.
His hoarse voice finds me every day
on the way to school and home again.
"Hey, Rabbit, whatcha doin'?"
A rock drops into my gut.
He walks next to me,
throws his elbow into my ribs
and edges me to the curb
hoping I'll take a swing at him.
I tried once and he flipped
me like a toy dog.

One day Jim, my best friend, gets fed up
with Nelson's jabs and taunts.
Someone on the playground yells "fight"
and a ring of kids surrounds them.
"Hit 'im, Jim."
"Take him, Nelson."
They shove back and forth
saying, "Yeah, Yeah, Yeah,
think you're big,
think you're tough."
Nelson takes a swing;
Jim catches his arm
and twists him to the ground;
the dust flies, the circle cheers.
Jim sits on Nelson
like we own the playground,
the school, and everything in it.

ELISABETH

A clump of boys
from fourth grade
stand on the playground
not speaking about
much of anything at all
until talk of love and girls
sneaks in from the edges
of somewhere.

"I love Elisabeth Lindberg,"
I say quickly, thinking
my early statement might
get me first dibs.

"So do I," says Jimmy.
"Me too," interrupts Robert.
"I've loved her ever since
first grade," argues Nicky.
"No, no," she knows I love her
shouts Paul, "I told her."
"You did!" we chorus.
"What did she say?"
"Nothing."

We sigh our relief
like the aaaaaaah
of a Pepsi
on a hot summer day.
And every once
in awhile we bunch
again on the playground
and speak of Elisabeth
as if our talk
makes love more possible.

The Desk

Mother buys
a cheap, wooden desk
painted bright orange
with two flimsy drawers
that rattle
when I pull them open.
There are two open shelves
on the side
which can hold
about twenty books.
Mother says, "You can have
this desk in your room
if you want it."

Before the desk came,
I only slept in my room,
made my bed,
picked up my dirty clothes,
and kept only my Sunday clothes
on a hanger in the closet.

I sit at the desk,
rub my hands over the surface,
pull open the top drawer,
and put a box of Crayolas
and a few pencils inside.
I shut the drawer
and I like the
sound of the thunk
that says the desk is mine.

I stand up beside the desk
and feel the silence of the empty shelves.
I pick up the four books I own,
run my fingers down the bindings,
and shelve them in alphabetical order.
Now I have a library in my room.

I sit down, pull open
the next drawer,
bigger and deeper
than the first.
There, I place my maps
of Europe, Asia, the United States,
and my stamp book
with stamps from the whole world.
Now, any place on earth is in my room.

Making Pies with Grandfather

Grandfather sings while he works;
his hands move slowly, peeling apples,
rolling dough, sprinkling sugar
and cinnamon until a pie
appears in the kitchen of his restaurant.

"Another bag of sugar, please."
I race to the storeroom
and plop it on the counter.
"My you're speedy."

He's short of apples
and I get the peeler,
place the apples
on two spikes, turn the crank,
watch the ribbons
of peel drop to the counter.
He laughs, "How did you know
how to use that machine?"

Six apple pies on the counter,
ready for the oven.
"I can't believe we've
made six pies before 7:00 A.M.
'Course, I've never had speedy
help like this before."
He lifts the handle
to the giant oven door,
a blast of hot air
strikes us in the face.
"Put on these mittens;
I think a boy who works so fast
is old enough to put pies in the oven."

Growing Pains

When we line up for gym,
I'm the last in line.
Even Tommy Crawford next to me
is an inch taller.
"Rabbits are always small,"
He says with a grin.

Mother says, "It's time
you saw a doctor."

"He's no smaller than me
when I was his age,"
my father argues.

"We've waited long enough.
We're going Monday."

I tell Jimmy I'm going
to the doctor.
He says, "They'll pull
your pants down, you know."

Dr. Seymour has a pretty nurse
and I know she'll be standing
there when he pulls my pants down.
She smiles, "Come right
this way, Donald."

"Not growin' huh,"
says Dr. Seymour.
"We'll see about that."
The nurse smiles
and stands there
holding a clipboard
with some papers on it.

"Put out your arms,
straight in front
of you like this."
Dr. Seymour has a tape
and he measures all my bones—
arms, legs, and feet.
"No worries here, Donald.
You'll grow, no doubt about it.
Go play baseball."
I smile at the nurse.

The Firemen

We have a red fire engine
with a bell on the front,
ladders on the side;
it's a toy you can sit in,
work the pedals,
but big enough to dream dreams
of fighting real fires.
We use hoses from Mother's washing
machine to put out blazes
in the shed, auto, and backyard.

We take turns being fire chief
and direct the others
in rescue operations,
pulling each other
to safety when the building tumbles.
We even save pets and babies from danger.

But we grow tired
of the imaginary
and in our dreams
we are more than kids at play.
We load sand into buckets
on the engine's tail
and my little brother
pedals the red machine
to Gorman's grassy field.

I light the match
while the crew waits
leaning over buckets of sand;
their eyes narrow
like seasoned fighters
to snuff the flames,
but a gust of wind
whips real red fire
past our buckets,
and the dry grass snaps
us awake, flowing now
like an angry yellow wave
toward the open field.

We beat on the flames
with our jackets.
Tears mix with soot
in the first burst of wind.
We cough and sputter
racing from one finger
of flame to another,
around a tree, along a wall.
We feel stupid
and imagine our parents' words,
the fire chief's anger.

The wind stops. We beat
out the last curling
licks of fire, slump down
to the ground, black
toasted field at our backs, and
begin the stories.

"Remember when it headed
for the big field?"
"Look at the holes in my jacket."
"I thought we were done for."
"Now that was a real fire."
"Your eyebrows
got burned white, Jim."
We giggle and roll
on the ground, punch
and poke our victory
until our stories
extinguish our fears.

Multiplication

My report card,
math, unsatisfactory.
I hate numbers;
they have to be just right.
People need to read;
They don't need math.

Mother sees Miss Adams, my teacher,
after school.
"You don't know
your multiplication tables;
We go to work after supper."

Mother has flash cards.
Questions on one side,
answers on the other.
Nine times three,
four times seven,
eight times eight.

I practice alone,
scratch Rags' head,
and leisurely turn the cards.
I miss my book.

Mother orders me
to the kitchen;
It's serious when we work
in the kitchen;
We sit on straight-back oak chairs.

She flashes the cards,
I have to speak fast.
Some I don't get.
Some I never get—
eight times seven,
nine times seven,
nine times three.

George looks over
my shoulder;
even my little brother
knows the right answers
before I do.
Rags looks sad
and leaves the room.

The Night Before Fishing Season Opens

After supper, Dad helps
George and me check supplies:
creel, bait tin, worms, pole,
rubber boots, not used
since last summer.
I see orange-bellied trout
dancing on the brook bank.

8:00 P.M.
Lay out my clothes
and wait for dawn;
burrowed into my pillow
hoping for sleep;
beneath the waterfall,
a pool boils
with hungry trout.

9:00 P.M.
Flip my pillow
to the cool side.
Cast my line
under the bridge, feel
the rat-a-tat of trout bites,
a quick jerk to set the hook.
I play the brookie to shore,
catch the speckled flash
of color before I swing
him to the bank.

9:40 P.M.
I imagine Mother's call
and smell the bacon;
bounce to the floor
and one by one I put on the clothes
from the neat pile
on the chair:
trousers, shirt, jacket.
I sit down,
slip on my long socks;
reach for my boots.

CHICKEN POX

Mother lifts my shirt
one June morning.
"What's this?" she says
pointing to red dots
on my stomach.
"Don't know."

She checks my back.
More red dots.
"I do believe it's
chicken pox.
Don't scratch."

I laugh.
"Hooray, no school
for the rest of the year."
I can play at home.
Read my books.

The second day more bumps
on my face,
behind my ears,
in my nose,
spots in my mouth.
I run a fever,
have nightmares,
walk in my sleep.

The itch.
Chains of heat
and burn crawl
like hairy caterpillars.
Don't scratch.
Don't scratch
or you'll have scars
for the rest of your life.

I run the tips of my fingers
over clusters of bumps
behind my ears.
The itch spreads up
my scalp, through my hair,
down my stomach
and along my legs.

I reach up behind my ears,
dig in my finger nails,
pull hard
and feel the delicious
warm water run
from the blisters
down my jaw
and along my neck.

The Winner

"King me, and watch."
George's hands move swiftly
as his king
jumps over three of my checkers.
Clunk, clunk, clunk.
He looks at me and grins.
"Okay, your move."

Day after day, I show
up for battle and lose:
checkers, Chinese checkers,
parchesi, baseball, shooting
baskets, poker, gin rummy, monopoly.

Steam pours from his ears;
intensity leaks from his eyes;
intelligence schemes far beyond
my dreamy notion of competition.

Once in a while I accidentally win;
George bellows, clears the board
with a swipe of his hand
sending chips and board pieces flying
against the wall,
rattling to the floor.
I am quiet and smugly smile
at my control.
It is my only victory.

Summer Squash

"Just a 'no-thank-you' helping,"
my mother choruses from the kitchen.
I sit alone at the table
with a mound of summer squash
on my plate; the kind of squash
with yellow warts, seeds, and white guts.
I lift the fork but my nose says,
"Smells like vomit" and I drop
the mass to my plate.

I sit alone, long after my brother
has eaten the cursed concoction.
He leaves with a grin
knowing I'll sit and suffer
until I eat one forkful.
Father and Mother look kindly
at Brother who loves vegetables
just because I don't.

Mother wants to finish
the dishes and raises a forkful
to my straight-lined mouth.
"Open up, now!" she orders.
The watery mash with seeds
and strings enters my mouth;
I prepare to swallow, push
my head forward, breathe
deeply, and hold the mix
in my mouth waiting
for Mother to leave.

I cough and spit the poison
to my plate and call my dog, Rags.
First, I give her two pieces
of meat and she begs for more.
I slip in a forkful of squash
in rhythm with her expectation.
She drops the bite to the floor,
shows the whites of her eyes,
then trots into the living room.

FIREWORKS

Fourth of July.
Firecrackers run rhythms
like rattlesnakes
in the hot sun.

The band marches
down Centre Street;
sun flashes from brass horns,
horses prance proudly;
old soldiers shuffle;
their medals puff pride.

We buy torpedos
at the firework's store;
six each — no more.
George slams them
on the sidewalk;
small explosions
announce his glee.
I save mine
to have fun
when he has none —
the torpedos nest
in my back pocket.

We eat lunch
at Grandpa's restaurant.
I spot a seat
in my favorite corner;
swiftly slide in
to a sudden explosion
from my back pocket —
gunsmoke fills the air
as customers jump to their feet
with me, shredded cloth hangs
from my trousers
as my bottom burns.

Mother checks the damage:
slight red marks
on my rear,
very red cheeks
on my face.
"Honestly, Donald."

Lost in a Book

We get up from the table
after a full lunch.
Dad says,
"Got a book here
you can have.
'Bout a kid lost
on a mountain in Maine.
True story.
Author signed it."

I reach for the book,
picture of a boy
on the cover
lying in a sack
thin and pale.

I open to the first page
and read standing;
Dad has disappeared,
leaving myself, the boy,
and the book.

I finally sit down,
and travel with the boy
up Mt. Katahdin, lost
in the clouds,
and I am the boy,
terrified, cold from the clouds,
bitten by blackflies,
mosquitos, following a brook, while I
eat blueberries.

I turn on
the living room lamp;
a bear moves from cover
and the boy watches
from the other
side of a blueberry bush.

"Time to set the table
for supper, Donald."
I hear the voice
but the boy trudges on and
loses his sneakers
in the rocky stream.
"Now . . . Donald!"
I want the voice
to tire, to go away.
The boy falls
in a heap
across the stream
from a cabin
where a man spots him.

"Will you put
that book away?
Honestly."

Learning to Ride a Bike

Mother buys two second-hand bikes.
Fifteen minutes after George
gets on his first bike,
he rides down the street.
Mother shows me
how to lift the pedal
on the right side,
push down with my right
foot, and pump.
She runs next to me
but every time
she lets go, I pedal
two times and fall over.

"Turn your wheel for balance,"
she shouts, "now the other
way, no not that way,
the other way."
I quit trying
while my little brother, George,
rides off to play ball
with his friends.
I stay home and read my book.

"Get out of the house
and try again,"
Mother orders.
I go through the same
routine, pedal twice,
lose balance, and dump
myself to the ground.

One night after supper
I play with friends
on their scooter
turn it this way and that,
spin down the sidewalk.
It is getting dark
but I pull my bicycle
out of the garage,
hop on and ride off.
The next day I ride
off to go fishing with Jimmy
while my book sits
on the desk in my bedroom.

The Lie

Mother is in the hospital
for an operation
and Grandma Sanderson
has come to take care of us.
She's strict.
If I'm two minutes
late from play,
she grips my wrist tightly
and swings me to a chair
to think about it.

I skin my knee
and get a deep cut.
She looks worried.
"When you go to school,
ask the nurse what to do."

On the way home,
I remember I've forgotten.
I know this is more serious
than being late from play.
I imagine a spanking,
early to bed for a week,
or extra work on Saturday.

She asks me what the nurse said.
"Wash it very carefully
with soap and water,
dry it, put on vaseline
and then place a band-aid over the top."
(That's what Mother
would have said,
except she'd use
iodine which stings.)

Rags Has Puppies

Mother announces,
"It's time for Rags
to have puppies.
I know just the dog
to be the father."

Mother explains
how the seed from the male
goes into Rags
so she'll have puppies.
Grandmother doesn't like
Mother to tell us such things.

The father is Teddy,
a long-haired brown dog,
who lives around the corner
from Grandmother.

I say I want
to watch
the seed go in.
"Nope, you'll make
her nervous.
She wants to be alone."

Rags begins
to grow fat.
I feel the puppies
move in her stomach;
she gives me funny looks.

Mother says it must be time —
Rags tried to make a nest
in the bottom drawer
in the back room.

The next night we go out
for a ride in the car;
Rags goes back and forth
on the seat
like she wants
to get out of the car.
Mother says, "I think
she must be in labor;
we'd better get home
in a hurry."

We rush to the house
but she has one puppy
on the lawn
and two more
in the drawer.

The puppies push away
at Rags' stomach
with their paws
to suck milk.
Rags growls
when we try to touch them.

Stealing Wood from Mr. Sweet

Each day after school
my brother and I walk by lumber
laid against the cemetery wall.
The wood doesn't seem
to belong to anyone.
The wood is in long thin strips
that look like scrap.
Each day we think maybe
we'd build a hut,
play war, cut out swords
or make ramps for our trucks.
We never see anyone using it.

So each day
we pick up a piece
and drag the long,
thin boards behind us.
No one says anything
or seems to mind.
We use the strips
as walls to guard
toy towns against invaders.

One day, I look out the window
and see Charley Sweet,
the man in charge of roads,
standing with our father.
He points at the wood
and my father's face
wears a frown and his mouth
is turned down.

We know we are in trouble.
Dad enters the house
and tells us to get outside
in a hurry.
It is hard to look
at Mr. Sweet.
He doesn't seem mad,
just shakes his big head
like he is very tired
and the world
is too much for him.

"You boys apologize to Mr. Sweet
for taking this wood,"
my father says.
I hang my head
and say, I'm sorry
in a low, mumbly voice.
"A little louder, please,"
my father says.
"This wood belongs to the town.
You take it back
where you found it
right this minute."

So, we move our army
trucks, tanks, and guns,
take down the walls
to our town,
and haul all those
pieces down the long road
until they are
lined up next
to the cemetery wall.

Snakes

Brown garter snakes
with yellow stripes
twine in and out
of the rough rocks
around the ledge
in our yard.

Each day I watch them
laze in the sun,
amble and slide
over each other,
then crawl back
into the cool crevices.

I pick them up
and they twine
around my wrist
or glide
up my arm.

Dad watches
with a frown.
The other day Rags
chased a six-foot
king snake through the brush;
Dad bombed
it with boulders.
He kept hitting the snake
until it was dead.

"These snakes bite you know.
Leave them alone."
I turn to argue,
"No, they don't."
The snake bites me,
leaving two red dots
on my thumb.

"And they don't
hurt either."

Weeding with Dad

I hear the rip, rip
of Dad's fingers tearing
at stubborn, wirey weeds.
I see his cap
just above the flowers,
catch a puff of smoke
from his pipe
as if an engine drives
him up and down the rows.

I think about my books,
a hut to build in the woods,
a ride on my bike with Jim,
playing baseball—
anything but weeds.

I can't hear Dad anymore;
He's out of sight,
down one row
and coming back the next.
I've done six plants
and I've got two full rows
to go before I escape this prison.

Doing Dishes

None of the other kids
have to do dishes.
Roy says that only girls do that.
Dad doesn't do dishes.

Mother says that George and I
will be good husbands
because we do dishes.
Maybe I shouldn't get married,
not even to Elisabeth Lindberg.

Thunderstorm

Rags trembles under the table
with the first sound of thunder;
the second boom sends
her panting into the bedroom
to lie on Mother's clothes.

Mother brings George and me
out to the screen porch
of our summer cottage.
Lightning pierces the dark
like silver darts,
rumbles follow.
I wonder if war
sounds the same.

"Start counting, one-one
hundred, two-one hundred
the second you see
the lightning flash,
then you'll know
how many miles away the storm is."

"When thunderstorms come,
your Aunt Helen draws
the shades and curtains
and jumps into bed,
even pulls the covers
over her head."

ZZZZZZZt - bang!
“That was right on top of us.”
We giggle our excitement.
Mother says, “I wouldn’t miss
this show and it doesn’t
cost a penny.”

HANDWRITING

Loops and circles,
circles and loops
march across my page
from left to right.

The class leans
into their pages
like factory workers;
heads go up and down;
Miss Fortin patrols
the aisles to check
our posture, the position
of our arms.

She looks at my page
of circles and loops
mixed with black smudges
and eraser holes.
She doesn't get angry;
she just lets out
a long, low sigh
like she wants to go home.

The Spanking

After supper on a warm June evening
when the sun sinks late,
George and I slip out of the house,
take off on our bicycles
with the clickety-click
of Rags following close behind.

The evening is quiet
and we are bold explorers,
cycling on streets unknown
down by the Bleachery,
a new development,
then across Route 1.

We feel the power
and range of our bicycles,
the openness of the early
evening in the dying light.
Rags trips faithfully along.

We turn for home,
thump up the steps,
open the door
to meet four blazing eyes,
open mouths, and angry teeth.
"Where have you been?"
"We were worried sick."
Rags dives under the couch.

Father's jaw is set;
his hand ready.
"Lean over my lap."
Mother says, "Not too hard."

I am determined not to cry,
seal my mouth.
Whack! Whack! Whack!
Dad's open hand strikes
my bottom, the clout
drives air out of my mouth,
the force begging for cries,
but I make no sound
get up, turn my back,
and walk out of the room.

Fishing for Conger Eels

I get to fish
with the men
after dark
because I am the oldest.
Dad says, "I think Don's
ready for it.
Won't be home until midnight."
George has to stay home;
He kicks at the door.

We fish for conger eels
off the rocks at Bonnet Shores.
The men have long hand lines
with lead sinkers,
hooks, and bait.
They twirl the line overhead
like cowboys after steers,
then let the line go
until we hear the splash
of the sinker in the dark.

Slowly, Dad pulls the line.
"Got a hit!"
I turn on the flashlight
and watch the line zig
and zag in the water.

"Charley, get the grabbers."
"Don, you hold the light."
Dad keeps pulling,
his face a ghost of wondering.
"Gettin' close now.
Everybody ready?"

We scurry to the water's edge,
our boots make hoarse, sandpaper
sounds across the barnacles.
The water boils,
a frenzy of commotion,
Dad pulls a six-foot eel
thrashing like a snake,
shaking its head,
teeth snapping.

"Get back, Don.
Look out for the teeth."
Charley holds two boards
like a pair of scissors,
then clamps them behind
the eel's head.
"Keep that light
right on the head."

Long white teeth
open and shut,
the head immobile,
but the rest of the blue,
slithery, black body
writhes, dances
and snarls line in a tangle
of foam and gunk.

"The sack, Don, the sack," Dad yells.
I balance light and sack,
Charley lifts the clamps high,
Dad and I guide the sack
beneath the body until
it drops into the burlap prison.
Dad says, "Good thing you were here, Don."

Last Touch

I tap my brother's shoulder;
"Last touch," I shout,
slam the door
race outside;
we weave through Gorman's
apple trees laughing.
He catches me,
"Last touch."
I chase him
to the house,
to the bathroom
where he locks the door.

After lunch, George
and Mother head downtown
in the car;
I reach through the open
window, "Last touch."
George's face
is a thundercloud.

After supper, I'm deep
in my book;
a man is on a liferaft
lost in the Pacific,
I feel no tap but hear a voice,
"Last touch, hah, hah."
George disappears on his bike.

Before bed, we brush
our teeth; I calculate
last touch for the day
and tap him with a laugh
as he heads
off with Mother
for a story;
he breaks from her grasp
and pounds me with his fist;
Mother yells, "Stop it you two, this minute.
I declare the game over and that's it."

Geography

We play the geography game.
Miss Adams pulls down a map,
any map in the world.
She says, "Find Ethiopia."
My hand is up first;
I whiz to the front
of the room and put
my finger on Ethiopia.

At home I shut my bedroom door,
pull out the bottom drawer
to my desk, and slowly turn
the Atlas pages.

Hour after hour I trace
rivers from source to sea,
hike through mountain passes,
green Amazon jungles,
visit capital cities,
and ride ocean liners
across the Atlantic
to England or France.

I beg for free road maps
at the corner Texaco station
and plot auto trips
to the White Mountains,
find the best way to a ballgame
at Fenway Park,
or imagine traveling
to Grandmother's house
for Christmas.

The Accident

One May morning
we hear the squeal of brakes.
"Oh no," my mother says;
she knows what the sound means.
Rags lies in the gutter;
she gets up on her front paws
when we run to her
but can't move the back ones.
Mother says, "Her back is broken;
we need to take her to the vet."
We are all crying,
even my Mom and Dad.

The vet says, "She can live
but she'll never walk again."
We talk it over, say goodbye
to Rags, and she licks my hand
through the wire cage
for the last time.
I can't stop crying.

The next day I take
my mother's evening purse
with jewels on the outside,
collect all Rags' hair
from the rug, in the corners
of the room, and under the couch,
rub it under my nose, sniff
it, cry some more
and put the purse
under some papers
in my desk drawer.

Not From Anywhere

"Everyone who has ancestors
from Italy raise your hands."
Michael Minetto and six
Italians raise theirs.
Miss Fortin is teaching
us about immigrants
who come to America.
I wonder what I'll do.

"Let's see, Sweden."
Davey Nichols, Elisabeth Lindberg,
Jean Ames, Terry Dahlquist
lift their hands.
Bobby Nelson puts up a fist.

"Ireland, how about Ireland?"
Jane Mullen, Roy Corr
and Agnes Scully
and a bunch of other kids.
"Yeah, Ireland,"
yells Pete Casey.
Only three kids
and me sit with our hands
on our desks.
I don't know where I'm from.
Grandpa, Grandma,
Great Grandpa, they're
all from here,
this country, America.

Miss Fortin addresses
the rest of us.
"Tell me where you are from
and then raise your hands."
"France," says Mike Fortier.
"Me too," Ellen Boudreau
raises her hand with a smile
and looks around the room.
"Should have thought
of that one," says Miss Fortin.
"My grandparents are from Germany
I think," says Rebecca Schmidt.
"And Donald?"
All eyes turn my way.
I can't think.
I simply don't know.
"Hah, he's not from anywhere,"
snickers Bobby Nelson.

GIGGLING IN CHURCH

Mrs. Densmore stands up to sing.
She has frizzy hair,
lots of lipstick
and a wide mouth.

She sounds like my grandmother
when she's gargling
in the bathroom
first thing in the morning.

I look at George.
He looks at me.
Mother looks at us.
Her eyes say, "Don't."

I look at George again.
He puts his hand
over his mouth
and begins to shake.
Water pours from his eyes.

My chest starts to build,
a force inside that grows
and fills, a laughing
bomb in there
that climbs up my throat
and blows out my nose.
“HAW,” it sprays.

A line of faces
as if pulled by strings,
turn like marionettes.

Muscles

In *Popular Mechanics* magazine
a man with rippling muscles
speaks from the page,
"I used to be a 98-pound
weakling but thanks
to Dynamic Tension,
I am a new person."

I weigh 56 pounds
and dream of defending
myself with pure muscle;
someday, I'll push Robert Nelson
into the street,
while Elisabeth Lindberg smiles.

On Being Sent to My Room

Each morning I hurry
through chores
before school:
dry the dishes,
dump the trash,
make my bed.

One day I skip chores;
I hope to finish them
when I come home.
Mother waits for me
when I come through the door.

"Why weren't the chores done?"
"Well, the day isn't over,
I'll do them now."
"Too late.
Go to your room and think it over."

I sit in my room,
read my book;
I cook a plan.
I won't come downstairs
not even for supper.

"You can come down now."
"I'm still thinking."
I read my book.
I have crackers
in my desk drawer.

"You can come down now;
time for supper."
"Nope, still thinking."
"You have five seconds
to be down these stairs,
one, two, three . . . ."

Faking It

Miss Johnson gives us fifty
math problems, a whole page
of misery that ruins
a perfectly good evening
of reading my book.

In the morning I wake
with forty math problems
staring at me.

At breakfast Mother says,
"Finish your cereal, Donald.
You'll be late for school."

Gradually my mouth fills
and I swallow nothing
until my cheeks bulge.
I spring from my seat, race
for the bathroom
and BLAH, I blow
the whole mess into the toilet.

"Ma, Ma," I yell.
"I've just thrown up."

Mother races in,
looks over my shoulder.
"You do that again
and I'll tan your hide."

The Big Field

Mr. Gammons mows the big field
with his tractor,
then rakes and bundles
hay for the barn.

George and I
grab our bats,
gloves, and balls
and race across the field
like major leaguers
in spring training.

We hit long flies
to each other
all afternoon,
never lose a ball
in the stubble,
and don't stop
until Mother calls
us for supper.

"Know what?
After supper,
let's make Fenway Park
in the big field."
We use a tape measure
and string to
lay out the infield,
step off the left field
foul pole, pound
in a stake
and mount crayon signs
on white paper,
316 FEET for left
420 to deep center,
and 302 for right.

I take a bat,
give the ball a good clout
and barely drop
one past second base.
George hits one to left field,
farther than mine,
but only into singles land.

We stand at home plate
and wonder if we'll
ever have muscles
that will rattle
one off the left field
wall in Fenway Park.

The Bark of Love

In fifth grade Miss Adams
moves Elisabeth Lindberg's seat
next to mine in the first row.
Even math is enjoyable after that.

I turn to catch her eye,
and linger in my gaze
to launch a dreamy stare.
I don't dare say "I love you,"
but I hope a doe-eyed
look will do.
When she glances back, I hold
her eyes, locking so tight
she can reel me across
the aisle to her seat.

I decide to speak to her
and send Katie, my emissary,
to arrange a meeting.
We meet by a tall maple tree
on the street
by her big yellow home
with the balcony on top.

We talk about stupid things
while I peel the bark
off the side of the tree
that stands between us.
I peek around the tree, talk,
peel bark, talk again,
until I finally blurt,
"I just want you to know
I love you."
She smiles and says,
"Thank you," and goes
back to her home.

EXPLORERS

In fifth grade we study
De Soto, Coronado,
Cortez, Pizzaro,
Ponce de Leon.

We trace their journeys
on maps in our history books.
Miss Adams leads us
through Florida swamps.
We discover the Mississippi,
travel across the southwest
without food and water,
and find treasure
in the temples of the Aztecs.

After school, Jim and I
change clothes, grab canteens,
knapsacks and hatchets
and discover the pond
down by the Bleachery.
We see Indians behind bushes,
follow a brook
to a larger stream
filled with fish,
then climb up on a boulder
and claim the land
for ourselves.